D1083723

HOW PLANT AND ANIMAL CELLS DIFFER

ANNA KASPAR
AND JUDY YABLONSKI

Britannica
Educational Publishing

Published in 2015 by Britannica Educational Publishing (a trademark of Encyclopædia Britannica, Inc.) in association with The Rosen Publishing Group, Inc. 29 East 21st Street, New York, NY 10010

Distributed exclusively by Rosen Publishing.
To see additional Britannica Educational Publishing titles, go to rosenpublishing.com.

First Edition

Britannica Educational Publishing
J. E. Luebering: Director, Core Reference Group
Anthony L. Green: Editor, Compton's by Britannica

Rosen Publishing
Executive Editor: Hope Killcoyne
Editor: Jeanne Nagle
Art Director: Nelson Sá
Designer: Nicole Russo
Photography Manager: Cindy Reiman
Photo Researcher: Karen Huang

Library of Congress Cataloging-in-Publication Data

Kaspar, Anna, author.
How plant and animal cells differ/Anna Kaspar and Judy Yablonski.—First edition.
    pages cm.—(The Britannica guide to cell biology)
Includes bibliographical references and index.
ISBN 978-1-62275-804-3 (library bound)
1. Plant cells and tissues--Juvenile literature. 2. Cell physiology--Juvenile literature.
3. Cytology—Juvenile literature. 4. Cells—Juvenile literature. I. Yablonski, Judy, author. II. Title.
QK725.K38 2015
571.6—dc23

2014030445

Manufactured in the United States of America

Cover: background © icholakov/iStockphoto.com; diagram silhouetted © Eraxion/iStockphoto.com

CONTENTS

INTRODUCTION

What do a dogwood tree, a daffodil, a duck, and a dragonfly have in common? If you said that they are all living things, you are right. Living things are called organisms. As you might guess, organisms can be divided into various groups. Dogwood trees and daffodils are plants, while ducks and dragonflies are animals. Plants are frequently green and generally rooted in the ground. They make and store the food they need to survive. Animals move around and need to eat food to survive.

Of course, plants and animals aren't the only kinds of organisms. For example, both mushrooms and the yeast we depend on to raise bread are fungi. Algae include a large variety of organisms, from those that appear as a green stain on damp rocks and tree trunks to those that form a fine scum on quiet ponds and the massive seaweeds that float in the ocean.

No matter what group organisms belong to, they are all made of cells. A cell is the smallest unit of living

Both this giraffe and the tree it is browsing on are organisms. Organisms can be found in every type of habitat on Earth—on land and in lakes, rivers, and oceans. Piotr Gatlik/ Shutterstock.com

yogurts. Unlike bacteria, animals and plants are multi-cellular, meaning they are made up of many cells. In fact, a single person or a tree contains many billions of cells.

The cells in multicellular organisms have certain recognizable parts in them. Each plant or animal cell has a nucleus, which serves as the cell's command center. It also has organelles, which are small, organ-like parts that have particular functions. While some organelles can be found in every kind of cell, others are found only in plant cells or animal cells. There are also other differences between plant and animal cells that make it possible to tell them apart.

While these differences are not terribly hard to spot, you'll need a good microscope to do so. Most cells are tiny. You might be able to see an unusually big plant or animal cell with your bare eyes, but you wouldn't be able to see any detail. Cells are so small that they are usually measured in microns (μm). A micron is equal to one millionth of a meter. There are about 25,000 microns in 1 inch.

Animals and plants are highly complex organisms. Not only do they consist of massive numbers of cells, but they are also made up of a variety of kinds of cells. Some of these cells are specialized, which means they are each suited to a particular job. For example, blood cells carry oxygen and carbon dioxide around your body. The wide variety of cell types allows each cell to do its specific job and contribute to the survival of the whole organism.

Groups of similar cells that work together to carry out a particular function are called tissues. For example, animals have muscle tissue, nerve tissue, and bone tissue, while plants have vascular tissues, known as xylem, and phloem. Together, many types of tissue work together to sustain a living organism.

CHAPTER 1

WHAT'S INSIDE A CELL?

Though they are different in some significant ways, plant and animal cells also have many things in common. Plant and animal cells are both eukaryotic. Eukaryotic cells contain a membrane-bound nucleus and organelles. The nucleus contains the cell's genetic material. Other cells, such as bacteria and archaea are prokaryotic, meaning that they lack organelles and a nucleus and their genetic material floats freely around the cell.

The organelles of eukaryotic cells are surrounded by membranes. These are like outer "skins" that filter material

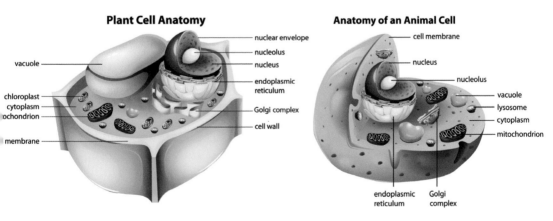

These side-by-side diagrams of a plant cell and an animal cell make it clear that the two kinds of cells contain many of the same organelles.
blueringmedia/iStock/Thinkstock

in and out of the organelles. Along with plants and animals, protozoa, algae, and fungi are all made up of one or more eukaryotic cells.

THE COMMAND CENTER

The nucleus is the command center of the cell. If a cell were an airplane, the nucleus would be the cockpit where the pilot sits. Located near the middle of the cell, the nucleus stores genetic information known as deoxyribonucleic acid, or DNA. The nucleus is wrapped in a double membrane that has pores, or holes, that let the genetic information pass from the nucleus to the rest of the cell. It is the largest structure in most animal cells and is clearly visible in both

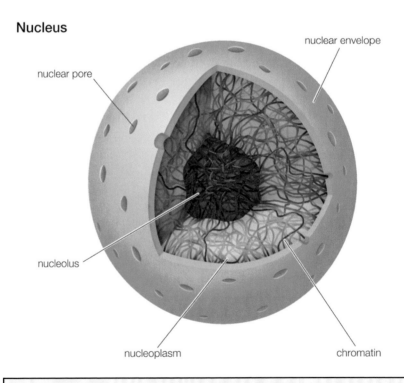

Nucleus

nuclear envelope

nuclear pore

nucleolus

nucleoplasm

chromatin

All eukaryotic cells contain a nucleus. Inside the nucleus is a syrupy nucleoplasm that contains the threadlike chromatin, which contains the cell's DNA. Encyclopædia Britannica, Inc.

plant and animal cells seen under a microscope. Inside the nucleus is a round body called the nucleolus. The nucleolus produces material known as ribonucleic acid (RNA) that is transported out of the nucleus to other parts of the cell.

The cell's organelles are controlled by information generated in the nucleus. The organelles each have their own specific role in keeping the cell alive. Some organelles make products for other cells to use, while others deal with waste and building materials.

KEY ORGANELLES

Most of the cell is made up a jellylike substance called cytoplasm. The cell's organelles float in the cytoplasm. A mesh-like network of fibers called the cytoskeleton criss-crosses the cytoplasm. It gives cells shape, anchors some organelles in place, and directs the movement of organelles. Because of its many varied functions, the cytoskeleton is often referred to as both the bones and the muscles of cells.

Ribosomes are tiny, round particles that synthesize proteins according to the instructions sent by the nucleolus. The proteins are then either used within the cell or exported outside of it. While ribosomes can be found scattered throughout the cytoplasm, they are often attached to the endoplasmic reticulum.

The endoplasmic reticulum (ER) is a network of membranous tubes and sacs. It twists through the cytoplasm from the cell membrane to the membrane surrounding the nucleus. The portions of the endoplasmic reticulum that contain ribosomes are called rough endoplasmic reticulum (RER). Areas of the network that do not contain ribosomes are called smooth endoplasmic reticulum (SER). The latter

Golgi apparatus

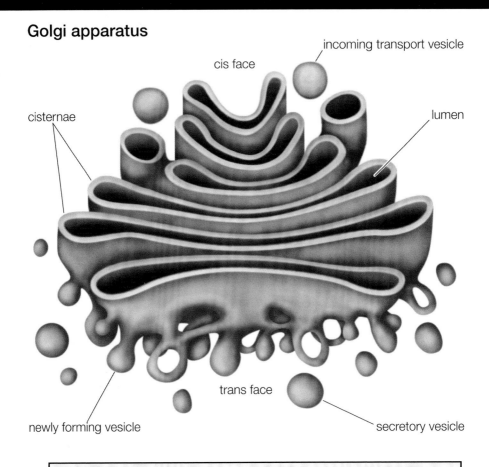

cis face

incoming transport vesicle

cisternae

lumen

trans face

newly forming vesicle

secretory vesicle

> *The Golgi complex, or apparatus, plays an important role in the modification and transport of proteins within the cell.* Encyclopædia Britannica, Inc.

is predominant in cells involved in detoxification or in the synthesis and metabolism of lipids.

The Golgi complex, or Golgi apparatus, is a membranous structure composed of stacks of thin sacs. Newly made proteins and lipids move from the RER and SER, respectively, to the Golgi complex. The materials are transported inside vesicles formed from the ER membrane. At the Golgi complex, the vesicles fuse with the Golgi membrane and the contents move inside the Golgi's lumen, or

LYSOSOMES

Lysosomes are round organelles in the cytoplasm that contain enzymes. Lysosomes combat harmful substances and help digest food, though they are more common in animal cells than in plant cells. Normally, the lysosomes do not release enzymes out into the cell itself. However, if a cell becomes damaged, the skins of the lysosomes disappear, enzymes are released into the entire cell, and the cell digests itself. This process of cell death is called necrosis.

center, where they are further modified and subsequently stored. When the cell signals that certain proteins are needed, the latter are "packaged" by the Golgi for export— part of the Golgi membrane forms a vesicle that then buds off, or breaks away, from the larger apparatus. The vesicle may migrate to the cell membrane and export its contents via exocytosis or it may travel to an intracellular location if its contents are needed by the cell itself. Lipids are processed by the same methods.

POWERHOUSES OF THE CELL

The large organelles that control cellular respiration for the cell are called mitochondria. During cellular respiration, glucose and oxygen react in the mitochondria to produce energy-storing molecules, known as ATP (adenosine triphosphate), that the cell needs to carry out its many functions. Because they are the sites of this important job, mitochondria are known as the powerhouses of the cell. Mitochondria are especially numerous in cells that use a lot of energy, such as liver and muscle cells.

Like the nucleus, the mitochondria have double membranes. The outer membrane is smooth, but the inner

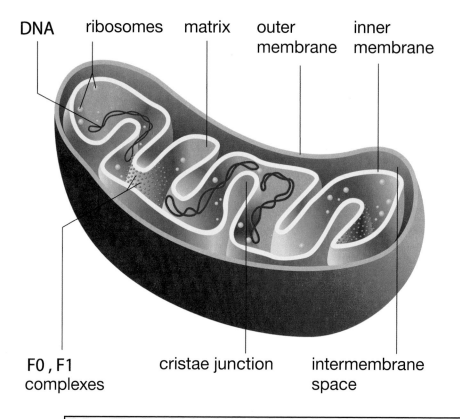

DNA ribosomes matrix outer inner
membrane membrane

F0 , F1 cristae junction intermembrane
complexes space

Mitochondria have inner and outer membranes, as well as their own DNA. The folds of the inner membrane are called christae, while the spaces within it are called the matrix. snapgalleria/Shutterstock.com

membrane has lots of wrinkles and folds. These wrinkles and folds increase the inner membrane's surface area. It is on the inner membrane that glucose reacts with oxygen to produce the primary energy for the cell.

THE PLASMA MEMBRANE

Both animal and plant cells are surrounded by a plasma membrane, though that membrane itself is surrounded by a cell wall in plant cells. The plasma membrane

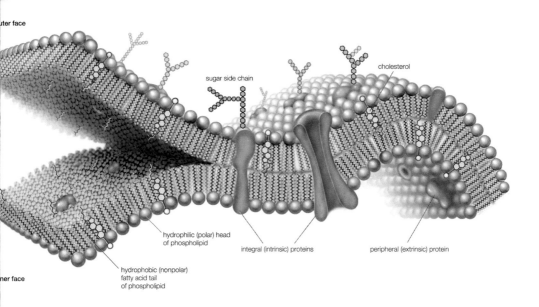

outer face

sugar side chain

cholesterol

hydrophilic (polar) head
of phospholipid

integral (intrinsic) proteins

peripheral (extrinsic) protein

hydrophobic (nonpolar)
fatty acid tail
of phospholipid

inner face

*Some molecules can freely move across the cell membrane. Other
molecules must cross the membrane through special protein channels.*
Encyclopædia Britannica, Inc.

serves as a protective coat. It also acts as a gatekeeper. It blocks some substances, but it lets others pass into and out of the cell. For example, the membrane allows the amino acids needed for building proteins and the carbohydrates needed for producing energy into the cell. The plasma membrane also regulates the amount of water inside the cell.

The plasma membrane is made up of two layers of lipid molecules. These lipid molecules hold proteins in place. The areas where the proteins lie mark the actual entrance and exit of molecules into the cell. Different proteins act as pathways for different molecules.

Similar membranes surround all of a cell's organelles. These membranes perform gatekeeper functions for the endoplasmic reticulum, the nucleus, the Golgi complex, and the mitochondria. Membranes divide regions of the cell into different compartments.

CHAPTER 2

SPECIALIZED ANIMAL CELLS

Animal cells are generally smaller than plant cells, which makes them harder to see under the microscope. They also lack the defined cell wall that plant cells have outside of their cell membranes, making their borders less distinct.

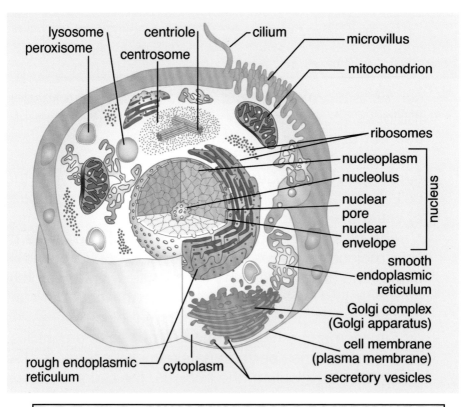

lysosome
peroxisome
centriole
centrosome
cilium
microvillus
mitochondrion
ribosomes
nucleoplasm
nucleolus
nuclear pore
nuclear envelope
nucleus
smooth endoplasmic reticulum
Golgi complex (Golgi apparatus)
cell membrane (plasma membrane)
secretory vesicles
rough endoplasmic reticulum
cytoplasm

This diagram shows the parts of a basic animal cell. Since animal cells lack the rigid cell wall found in plant cells, they have less rigid shapes. © Merriam-Webster Inc.

Animals have many kinds of specialized cells. These are cells that are modified to carry out a particular function, such as transporting a certain substance or executing a specific task. One example of specialized cells in animals is the red blood cells in mammals, which transport oxygen from the lungs to all of the body's tissues and contain hemoglobin, an iron-rich protein that binds oxygen. Another example is the choanocytes, or collar cells, that line the central cavities of sponges, capture food particles, and absorb oxygen from the water current. Each collar cell has a flagella, a tiny whiplike structure that creates a current to help draw the water through the sponge.

NEURONS

One trait that makes animals special is their ability to respond quickly to internal or external stimuli. For example, you can spin around if you hear a crash behind you. The system that coordinates these responses is the

Her sensory neurons let this girl hear the water's lapping noises, feel her dog pulling on its leash, and see everything around her. Elena Elisseeva/ Shutterstock.com

nervous system. In vertebrates, or animals with backbones, the nervous system depends on nerve cells, also known as neurons.

Neurons are very long and thin. They have wirelike extensions, along which nerve signals pass from one part of the body to another. Though neurons are thinner than thread, some can be as long as 3 feet (0.9 meters).

Much like telephone wires that are connected in a network and transmit messages, neurons carry messages over a network that stretches throughout an animal's body. For many animals, including humans, the centers of this network are the brain and the spinal cord.

Animals have sensory neurons and motor neurons. Your sensory neuron cells allow you to feel sensations, such as pressure, heat, cold, or pain, by carrying messages from such places as your eyes or your ears to your

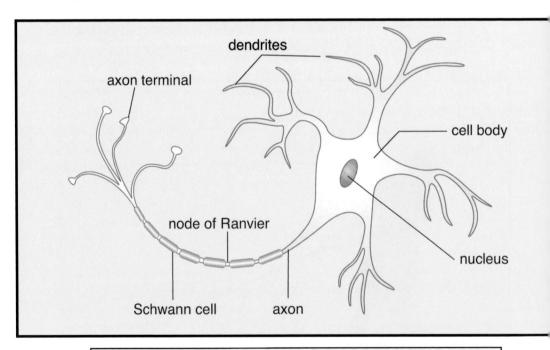

This diagram shows a neuron. Dendrites receive and conduct impulses to the cell body, where inputs arriving from various dendrites are integrated. © Merriam-Webster Inc.

brain. Your motor neurons carry messages from your brain and spinal cord to other parts of the body to tell these body parts to react by moving the right muscles in your arms, legs, or eyes.

Interneurons connect sensory neurons to motor neurons. If you accidentally touch a hot stove, all three types of neurons will work together to immediately send a message to your hand, "Remove from hot stove now!" Nerve cells are connected to each other in long chains by branchlike dendrites at one end of each nerve cell and a long axon at the other end, which transmits the message to the neighboring cell's dendrites. The chains of nerve cells carry messages from neuron to neuron, until a message reaches its appropriate destination.

MARROW AND MORE

While not every animal has bones, the only organisms that have bones are animals. Bones are made up of bone cells. The most common kind of bone in the human body is compact bone. In compact bone, the cells are arranged in concentric circles. This means there are many circles within circles. They look like the concentric circles you see when you cut a slice of an onion.

Although a bone is very hard, it is actually hollow inside. It is filled with red and yellow cells, which make up the bone marrow. The bone marrow is where blood cells are made. The red bone marrow cells make red blood cells, while the yellow bone marrow cells make white blood cells.

There are several types of bone cells. Some bone cells make new bone cells. These bone-building cells allow your bone to repair itself if it breaks. Other bone cells actually consume bone from the inside. These self-consuming bone cells ensure that your bones remain hollow on the inside so that bone marrow has room to grow. As you grow from childhood to adulthood, your bones must grow, too. Therefore, the space in the hollow area of your bones must get bigger in order to make more space in the inside of the bone. Thanks to the bone-eating cells, your bones continuously make room for the bone marrow that makes your blood cells, even as your body grows bigger.

RED BLOOD CELLS

Red blood cells are the most common kind of blood cell. One of a red blood cell's main jobs is to carry oxygen from the lungs to the rest of the body, where it is used in cellular respiration. The other is to carry the carbon dioxide that is created by cellular respiration away from the cells. The red blood cells carry carbon dioxide to the lungs, from which you breathe it out.

MUSCLE TISSUE

A group of muscle cells together forms muscle tissue. Individual muscle cells are long and thin. They can shorten or lengthen (contract and release) to allow for movement. You know how tired you sometimes feel after running? That is because your muscles use up a lot of energy every time they have to contract and release. Because they use so much energy, muscle cells have a lot of mitochondria.

The mitochondria provide a site in the cell for oxygen to combine with glucose in the process of cellular

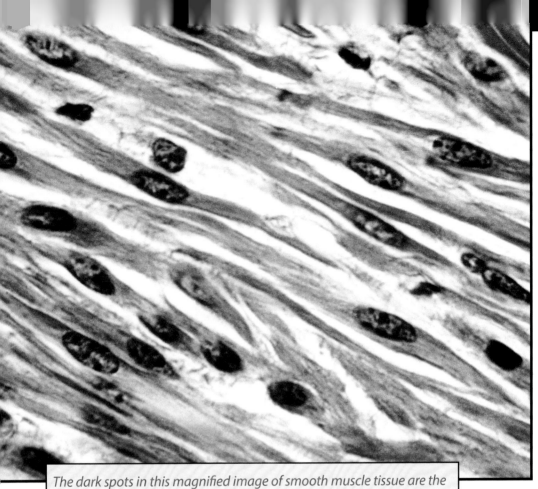

The dark spots in this magnified image of smooth muscle tissue are the cells' nuclei. Smooth muscle movement is controlled by the autonomic nervous system and cannot be controlled consciously. BIOPHOTO ASSOCIATES/Photo Researchers/Getty Images

respiration. This combination produces the energy needed for the cell to carry out its functions. A person who moves a lot, such as an athlete, appears to have larger muscles. This is because his or her muscle cells are getting bigger. The athlete's body self-regulates itself to make sure that its muscle tissue will have enough mitochondria to keep up with all the movement the athlete demands of his or her body. Conversely, a body that remains idle experiences the reverse process.

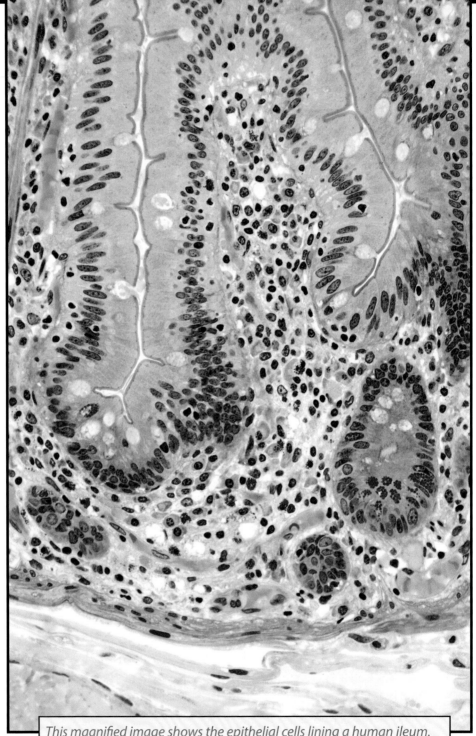

This magnified image shows the epithelial cells lining a human ileum. The ileum is a portion of the small intestine. Visuals Unlimited, Inc./Dr. Gladden Willis/Getty Images

EPITHELIAL TISSUE

Epithelial tissue can be found on both the outside of an animal's body and the lining of its organs. Epithelial cells can be found in an animal's intestines, lungs, skin, and blood vessels. In fact, all the organs in an animal's body are covered with epithelial cells. They come in all different shapes. Some epithelial cells are flat, while others are cube shaped or columnar.

The epithelial cells lining the insides of the intestines allow digested food to pass through and into the blood. The many air sacs in the lungs, called alveoli, are also lined with epithelial cells. The lining of the alveoli is extremely thin so that gases, such as oxygen, can pass freely through it and be absorbed by red blood cells.

The insides of blood vessels are lined with a type of epithelial cells called squamous epithelial cells. Squamous cells have the appearance of thin, flat plates. The shape of these cells allows the inside of blood vessels to be very smooth so as to allow blood to flow easily without the blood cells becoming damaged.

As is the case with all animals, your whole body is wrapped in a covering of epithelial cells. Your outer layer of skin, called the epidermis, is made up of epithelial cells that are flat, hard, and tough. The skin cells protect the body parts beneath from germs and other environmental hazards. A break in the skin, such as a cut, allows germs to get inside and possibly cause an infection.

You lose epithelial cells from your skin every minute of every day. Every time you wash your hands or rub your skin, you lose some epithelial skin cells. However, they regenerate themselves so quickly that you never even notice. In fact, you lose up to 5 pounds (2.3 kilograms) of dead skin cells every year!

CHAPTER 3

PLANT CELL PARTS

Plant cells are much easier to see under a microscope than animal cells for two reasons. The first reason is that plant cells are generally larger than animal cells are. In addition, plant cells have thick cell walls outside the plasma membranes, which makes them easy to identify. Animal cells have only thin, flexible cell membranes. A plant's thick cell wall is made of a rigid substance called cellulose, which helps the plant cell maintain its shape. Cellulose also protects the plant cell from mechanical damage. Cellulose is made up of linked glucose units. It is the major raw material component used in the production of certain manufactured fibers, such as rayon. Historically, paper was produced from cotton plants, which are 91 percent cellulose. Today, hardwoods and softwoods provide the major source of papermaking fibers, which are only about 60 percent cellulose.

Though they have numerous organelles and a nucleus, plant cells are primarily composed of a large central vacuole, which fills at least 80 percent of a mature plant cell. The vacuole is a large watery bag near the center of a cell. It stores chemicals and waste products that would be dangerous to the cell if they built up in the cytoplasm.

Plant cell

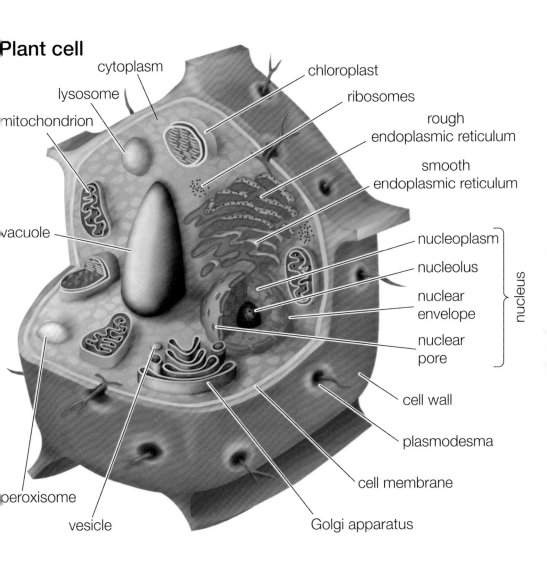

cytoplasm

lysosome

mitochondrion

chloroplast

ribosomes

rough endoplasmic reticulum

smooth endoplasmic reticulum

vacuole

nucleoplasm

nucleolus

nuclear envelope

nuclear pore

nucleus

cell wall

plasmodesma

cell membrane

peroxisome

vesicle

Golgi apparatus

Like animal cells, plant cells have a cell membrane, cytoplasm with a variety of organelles, and a nucleus. Unlike animal cells, they also have a rigid cell wall and feature large vacuoles and chloroplasts. Encyclopædia Britannica, Inc.

VACUOLES

The large central vacuole and the thick cell wall work together to aid the growth process for the entire plant. Most plant growth occurs when the large central vacuole and the cytoplasm absorb water. By absorbing water, plant cells elongate, or grow longer. By contrast, animal cells grow by synthesizing organic molecules and increasing their cytoplasm. When the vacuole absorbs water in plant cells, it expands the contents of the cells within the cell walls, causing the plant to become stiff and have turgor pressure. If there is not enough water in the vacuoles, the plant will wilt.

Transpiration is the process in which water passes through a plant. The outer cells of the leaves are constantly losing water through evaporation. This is especially true on a hot, sunny summer day when water evaporates quickly. When this occurs, the plant cell's vacuoles shrink because they are losing water. Therefore, the concentration of

WHY DO PLANTS WILT?

If a plant does not absorb enough water, it wilts. When you see your plant leaves drooping, it is because the turgor pressure in its cells has dropped and the cells can no longer support the plant. After a while, the plant will start to die and will undergo plasmolysis. In this process, the vacuoles of the plant cells shrivel and pull the cytoplasm away from the cell walls, causing the plant to lose strength and die.

minerals and sugars in the vacuoles of leaf surface cells becomes higher than the concentration of sugars in the vacuoles of cells inside the leaf, which are not near the warm surface. Water then travels from the inner cells with a higher concentration of water to those on the surface with a lower concentration of water. This causes more water to be pulled up through the stem and roots. This process of transpiration occurs constantly. However, the rate varies depending upon how much water is in the soil.

CHLOROPLASTS

Unlike animal cells, plant cells and certain types of algae contain chloroplasts. These organelles contain a green pigment called chlorophyll. All green parts of the plant contain chloroplasts, including the stem, the leaves, and, sometimes, unripe fruit. During the process of photosynthesis, the chlorophyll molecules in the chloroplasts capture light energy from the sun and store it in a chemical form. Photosynthesis provides energy for all living things in the form of glucose.

The pigment in the chloroplasts, known as chlorophyll, traps the light energy. If you have ever worn a black shirt on a very sunny day, you know that dark colors absorb more light than light colors. You most likely felt warmer than normal because the more pigment a substance has, the more light it will trap.

Chloroplasts belong to a group of organelles, known as plastids, which are found in the cytoplasm of plant cells. Chromoplasts are another type of plastid. They contain pigments called carotenoids, which give fruits, flowers, and autumn leaves their orange and yellow hues. Carotenoids can be a variety of colors, while

Chloroplast

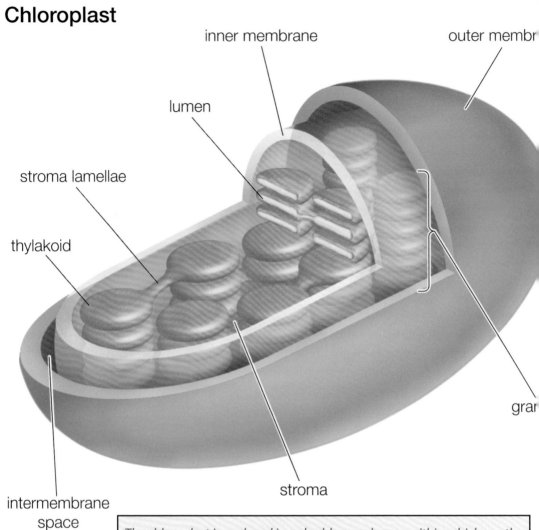

inner membrane

outer membr

lumen

stroma lamellae

thylakoid

grar

intermembrane space

stroma

> The chloroplast is enclosed in a double membrane, within which are the stroma (a matrix containing dissolved enzymes) and the lamellae (internal membranes folded into closed disks, the thylakoids).
> Encyclopædia Britannica, Inc.

chlorophyll is always green. Sometimes, chloroplasts will convert into chromoplasts. When this occurs in fruit, the color changes from green to a color

FALL FOLIAGE

Chlorophyll, the green pigment inside the chloroplasts, absorbs red and blue light rays from the sun, and it reflects green light rays. This is why leaves are green. In autumn, the chlorophyll in most plants breaks down. Other pigments, such as carotene and tannin, become more abundant. These other pigments reflect orange, yellow, and brown light, making the leaves display a stunning array of fall colors.

Some of the pigments that make fall foliage so colorful are the orange carotenes and the yellow xanthophylls. Jeremy Woodhouse/Stockbyte/Getty Images

characteristic of that fruit. This color change is a sign that the fruit is ripe and ready to eat.

Some plant cells contain more chloroplasts than other plant cells. The amount of chloroplasts is determined by the position of the cells inside the plant. Since

Cacti adapted to live in places with little water. Given that most water loss in plants happens through the leaves, the leaves of cacti have been reduced to form the protective spines. Oleg Znamenskiy/Shutterstock.com

leaves are the main sites of photosynthesis, cells on the inside of the leaves contain the most chloroplasts. In most plants, the flat surface of the leaves provides a large area for sunlight absorption. The chloroplasts of cacti are located in the green spongy stem rather than

the leaves (which have been modified to form the cactus spines) and photosynthesis thus occurs there.

CHAPTER 4

SPECIALIZED PLANT CELLS

Most plants are vascular plants, meaning they have leaves, roots, and stems. The leaves, roots, and stems work together to gather nutrients, anchor the plant, and transport food, nutrients, and water. Plants that are nonvascular include mosses and liverworts. Nonvascular plants perform all of these same functions without true stems, roots, leaves, or vascular tissues.

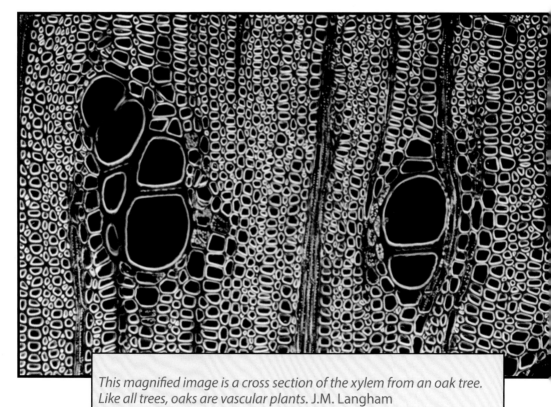

This magnified image is a cross section of the xylem from an oak tree. Like all trees, oaks are vascular plants. J.M. Langham

Vascular plants have vascular tissue running up and down their stems. Vascular tissue carries fluids and helps support the plant. If you have ever seen a cross section of a tree stump, you can easily see the vascular tissue that makes up the transport system of vascular plants.

XYLEM AND PHLOEM

Vascular tissue is made up of both xylem tissue and phloem tissue. Xylem tissue carries water and minerals up through a plant from the roots to its branches and leaves. Phloem tissue distributes food made in the leaves to all parts of the plant. Both of these tissues can be found in the stems of plants. The stem, therefore, serves as the transportation system for the plant. The stem is like a two-way highway from the soil to the surface of the leaves and back.

Xylem cells are long, hard walled, tube shaped, and joined from end to end. When they die, their contents dissolve. The cells then become microscopic tubes through which water flows to reach the different parts of the plant. Although plants do not have bones, their xylem keeps them firm. The wood we get from tree trunks is made up of xylem tissue. The stalk of a flower and even a blade of grass also contain xylem, which helps keep them upright. In these smaller plants, water also plays a large role in keeping the stalk stiff and tall. In small plants, turgor pressure, which is created when the large central vacuoles of the plant cells absorb water, also helps keep the plant upright.

Phloem cells form long tubes for conveying food-rich sap manufactured in the leaves to other parts of the plant. They tend to be found nearer to the outside of a trunk or stem than xylem are. Some plants have a layer of pith at the very inside. Pith tissue is used for storing food.

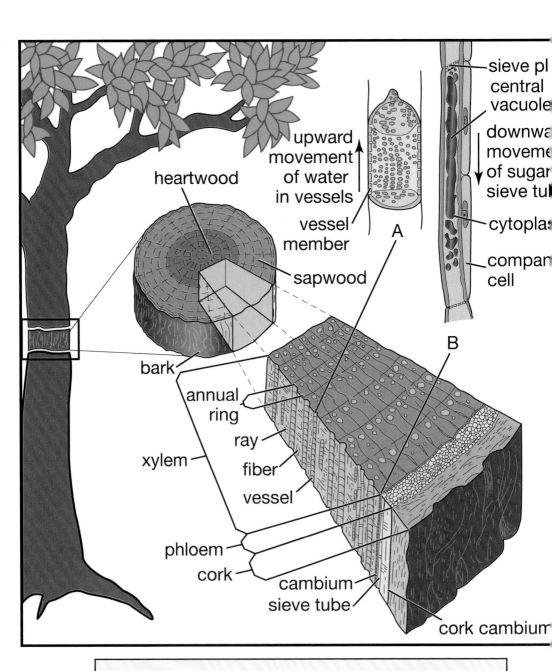

sieve pl
central
vacuole

downwa
moveme
of sugar
sieve tu

cytopla

compan
cell

upward
movement
of water
in vessels

heartwood

vessel
member

sapwood

A

B

bark

annual
ring

ray

xylem

fiber

vessel

phloem

cork

cambium
sieve tube

cork cambium

Vascular tissue is organized into strands called vascular bundles, each containing xylem and phloem. In stems, the vascular tissue is organized into many vascular bundles. Encyclopædia Britannica, Inc.

WAXY STEMS OR BARK

The outside of a green leaf or stem is covered with a layer of cells called the epidermis. The cells of this outer layer make a waxy substance, which acts as a smooth, waterproof coating for the plant. In herbaceous, nonwoody stems, this coating allows the stem to fill up with water and makes it stiff and upright. The epidermis consists mainly of parenchyma (packing tissue) and collenchyma (supporting tissue).

GROUND TISSUE

Plant tissues are said to be simple if they are composed of a single type of cell and complex if they are composed of two or more cell types. The complex tissues include the dermal and vascular tissues of plants. Simple tissues, also referred to as ground tissues, include parenchyma, collenchyma, and sclerenchyma.

Parenchyma tissue, while found throughout the plant, is particularly abundant in the stems and roots. The leaf cells that carry out photosynthesis are also parenchyma cells. Unlike many other plant cells, parenchyma cells are alive at maturity and retain the ability to divide.

Like parenchyma cells, collenchyma cells are alive at maturity. They differ from parenchyma cells in that they have thick cell walls. Collenchyma tissue is most often found in the form of strands or cylinders of cells in stems and leaves. The thick cell walls of collenchyma cells provide support to these plant structures. The strands of tissue in celery are collenchyma tissues.

Sclerenchyma tissue is found throughout the plant. The cells of this tissue also have thick cell walls. These walls are often composed of the substance lignin, which gives the walls a great deal of strength. At maturity the cells die, but their cell walls remain intact. Sclerenchyma cells give plant parts strength and support.

The woody stems of trees have an outer protective layer of tough bark. Year by year, new vascular tissue forms, increasing the diameter of the tree trunk. If you have ever looked at the inside of a tree trunk, you have probably seen a number of concentric circles. Each year new layers of xylem are produced. Large xylem cells are produced in the spring and are lighter in color. The production rate of new cells slows during summer, producing smaller, darker xylem cells. The changes in the size of xylem cells produced during varying seasons produce annual rings. The number of these concentric circles is a good indicator of the age of a tree.

THE STOMATA

A leaf consists of a thin, flat blade, supported by a network of veins, a leaf stalk called a petiole, and a leaf base where the leaf joins the stem. Stomata are tiny openings in the epidermis through which the exchange of water and gases takes place. They are mainly found on the underside of leaves and are composed of pairs of specialized guard cells.

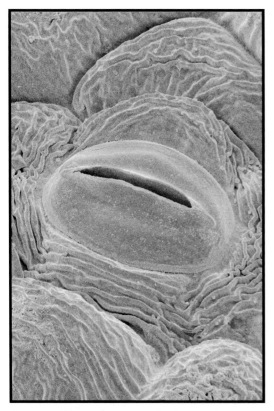

This magnified image shows a stoma on the underside of a leaf from a camellia plant. Susumu Nishinaga/Science Photo Library/ Getty Images

There are thousands of guard cells on the underside of each leaf. The guard cells come in pairs and look like two tiny kidney beans, placed side by side so that there is a small hole in the middle.

Inside View of a Root

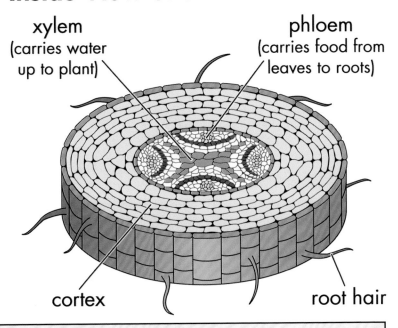

xylem
(carries water up to plant)

phloem
(carries food from leaves to roots)

cortex

root hair

> *In this cross section of a typical root, the primary xylem and the primary phloem can be seen arranged in a central cylinder.* Encyclopædia Britannica, Inc.

The structure of the guard cells allows them to perform their special function. The guard cells open and close depending on whether they are letting in water or gases in the air. It is through these openings that the plant breathes.

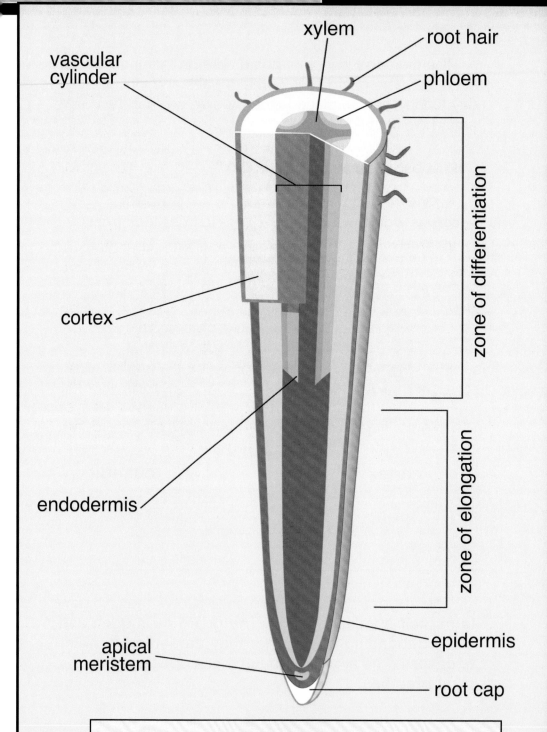

The root cap is at a root's tip, with cell division happening just above it. Next comes the zone of elongation, in which cells grow. The zone of differentiation contains fully functional cells. © Merriam-Webster Inc.

THE ALL-IMPORTANT ROOTS

Much like the epithelial cells that line the intestines of animals and aid in digestion, the root cells of plants help them absorb nutrients. Roots anchor a plant in the soil and absorb water and minerals. The roots' absorptive properties are increased by root hairs, which grow behind the root tip, allowing the maximum amount of surface area for absorption.

A carrot is the root of a carrot plant. When you look at round carrot slices in a salad, you can see an inner core that is a slightly different color than the outer core. These two sections contain different kinds of cells. Roots have an outer epidermis layer, a cortex of parenchyma tissue, and a central cylinder of vascular tissue.

Meristem cells, located near the tip of the root, divide to produce new cells. This elongation of the cells pushes the root farther down into the soil. A layer of cells called the root cap, which covers the tip of the root, protects the root tip as it grows down.

CHAPTER 5

MAKING AND BREAKING DOWN FOOD

Cells are the sites of two processes without which life as we know it could not exist: cellular respiration and photosynthesis. Cellular respiration occurs in the mitochondria of both plant and animal cells. It provides the energy that cells need to perform their functions. Photosynthesis produces the sugars that are broken down in cellular respiration. Though photosynthesis cannot happen in animal cells, animals depend on the process to produce the food they eat. Photosynthesis not only provides food for animals, it also generates the oxygen that they breathe.

STORING LIGHT ENERGY

Plants are Earth's natural solar panels. They capture the energy of sunlight and store it as chemical energy, in the form of the sugar glucose. Sugar and sunlight are not the only components in the photosynthesis process, though.

The process requires water and the gas carbon dioxide. Along with the sugar glucose, it also produces the gas oxygen. The chemical equation for the photosynthesis reaction looks like this:

$$6CO_2 + 6H_2O + energy \rightarrow 6O_2 + C_6H_{12}O_6$$

The equation may look confusing, but it is actually quite simple. CO_2 is the formula for carbon dioxide. A carbon dioxide molecule has one atom of carbon (abbreviated C) and two atoms of oxygen (abbreviated O). A water molecule is referred to as H_2O because it is made

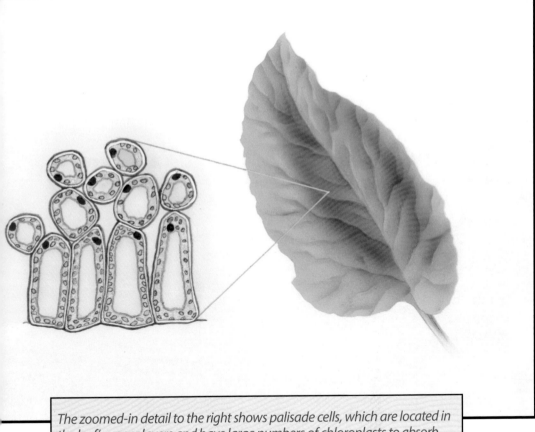

The zoomed-in detail to the right shows palisade cells, which are located in the leaf's upper layers and have large numbers of chloroplasts to absorb incoming light. Richard Ward/Thinkstock

up of two atoms of hydrogen (abbreviated H) and one atom of oxygen. The equation for photosynthesis shows that each individual reaction requires six carbon dioxide molecules, six water molecules, and some sunlight energy to produce six molecules of the gas oxygen (O_2) and one molecule of the sugar glucose ($C_6H_{12}O_6$).

Carbon dioxide enters the leaf by way of the stomata, flanked by its two guard cells. Oxygen exits the plant through the stomata in the leaves as a waste product of photosynthesis. An extensive network of xylem tissue brings water into the leaves, while phloem tissue transports glucose produced by photosynthesis from the leaves to the rest of the plant. Plants use some of the glucose they make in photosynthesis for cellular respiration. The rest of it is stored, sometimes in the form of glucose and sometimes in the form of more complex carbohydrates, or sugars.

The process of photosynthesis allows plants to be self-feeding, or autotrophic. Autotrophs sustain themselves without eating other organisms as humans and other animals do. However, they do still need the sun's light energy, carbon dioxide from the air, and water and minerals from the soil.

Given that photosynthesis consumes carbon dioxide, many scientists are against deforestation and advocate for the restoration of forests as a means to slow global warming. Global warming is an ecological crisis caused by unusually high levels of carbon dioxide and other greenhouse gases in the atmosphere. The greenhouse gases trap heat near the surface of Earth, which has caused a rise in average temperatures over the past century. Scientists have suggested that more forests would amount to more plant cells requiring carbon dioxide for photosynthesis. This would leave less carbon dioxide in the atmosphere.

While deforestation, or the cutting down of forests, is a problem in many places, there are a few areas, such as New England, where forests are actually growing back. Panoramic Images/Getty Images

USING GLUCOSE

Animals could not undergo cellular respiration without the glucose and oxygen produced by plants during photosynthesis. Animals get glucose by directly eating plants (herbivores) or by eating animals that ate plants (carnivores). Often animals eat complex molecules that get broken down into glucose, rather than consuming glucose itself.

Along with glucose, cellular respiration requires oxygen. The respiration process takes place in the mitochondria. While photosynthesis traps light energy in the form of chemical energy, the cellular respiration process releases energy. In addition to the energy it produces, cellular respiration also generates carbon dioxide and water. Cellular respiration is basically the opposite of photosynthesis, as you can see by looking at the equations for the two processes. The equation for the photosynthesis is:

$$6CO_2 + 6H_2O + sunlight \rightarrow C_6H_{12}O_6 + O_2$$

While the equation for cellular respiration is:

$$6O_2 + C_6H_{12}O_6 \rightarrow 6CO_2 + 6H_2O + energy$$

As you can see in the second equation, each individual cellular respiration reaction uses six oxygen molecules and a glucose molecule to produce six carbon dioxide molecules, six water molecules, and a new form of energy.

The processes of photosynthesis and cellular respiration are inextricably linked. The by-products of

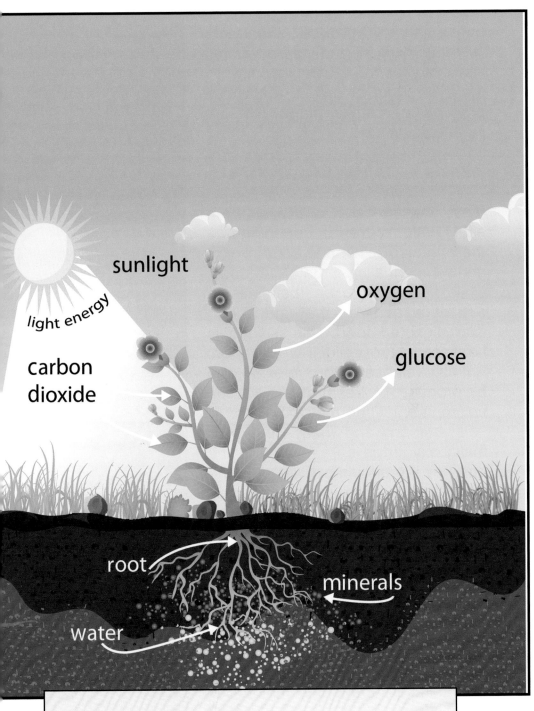

This diagram shows both what plants require and what they produce.
snapgalleria/iStock/Thinkstock

photosynthesis provide organisms with the oxygen and carbohydrates necessary for cellular respiration, while the by-product of cellular respiration provides the carbon dioxide needed for photosynthesis.

OXYGEN TRANSPORTATION

Most animals take in oxygen from either water or the air, depending on the organism. Humans take in oxygen when inhaling air into our lungs, while fish depend on their gills to extract oxygen from the water. Along with digested food, this oxygen is necessary for cellular respiration. Animals release carbon dioxide, the by-product of respiration, to the environment when they exhale.

In humans and many other animals, oxygen is spread around the body by the circulatory system. The circulatory system is made up of a vast network of branching blood vessels. All the cells in the body require a constant supply of oxygen. Each cell has a tiny blood vessel running right by it. This is so that oxygen can be carried to the cells by the bloodstream and carbon dioxide can be carried away. Like a circle, the system has no beginning or end. It takes about one minute for

Adult frogs get the oxygen they need by breathing air into their lungs. However, frogs begin their lives as tadpoles, which have gills to absorb oxygen. Bill Kennedy/Shutterstock.com

your blood to make a complete loop around the circulatory system.

Mammalian lungs have a huge surface area to receive the maximum amount of oxygen possible from each inhale. The lungs have branchlike air tubes, the bronchi and bronchioles, which allow for the most possible exposure to oxygen. The bronchioles dead-end in microscopic air sacs called alveoli, which have a moist coating that dissolves the oxygen. A layer of epithelial tissue lets the oxygen pass through to the capillaries through which the oxygen is carried by blood flowing through vessels to every cell of the body.

GILLS

Most fish breathe by means of gills. They consist of many tiny filaments supplied with blood vessels. Water enters the open mouth. Then the fish closes its mouth and the water is forced over the filaments and out through the opercula. Oxygen dissolved in the water is absorbed into the bloodstream through the delicate membrane of the filaments. Inside the mouth are straining devices called gill rakers. They prevent food and debris from passing over and injuring the gills.

The red blood cells carry oxygen through the body and drop it off at other cells. Then they pick up carbon dioxide and carry it back to the lungs. Mammals then breathe out the carbon dioxide into the air. As with all cells, the red blood cells' shape helps the cells to perform their function. The red blood cells' disk shape makes it easy for them to carry oxygen to, or carry carbon dioxide away from, cells.

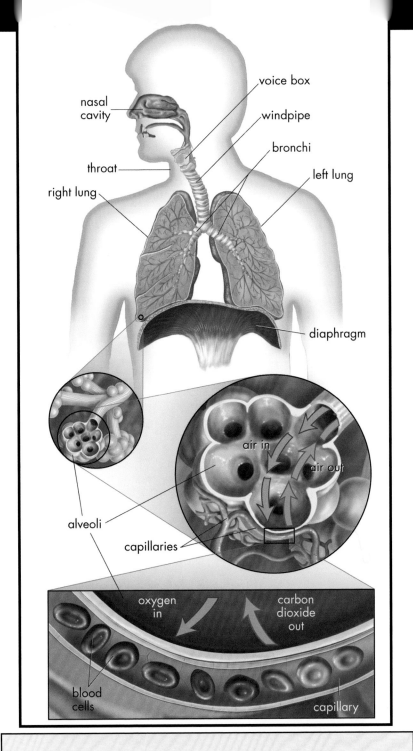

This diagram shows how the alveoli and capillaries in the lungs exchange oxygen for carbon dioxide. Encyclopædia Britannica, Inc.

INTERDEPENDENCE

Plants and animals must coexist in order for either to flourish. This fundamental relationship comes from the need of every cell to survive. In addition to the relationship of photosynthesis and cellular respiration, the

Here, a cactus wren sits on a saguaro cactus. Cactus wrens eat fruit from cacti and other plants, as well as bugs that feed on plants. In turn, the birds spread the plants' seeds far and wide. tntphototravis/ Shutterstock.com

interconnection between plants and animals can be found in many other ways. Examples include how bees help pollinate flowers while they get nectar and how animals help disperse seeds by eating them or getting them stuck in their fur or paws.

The interdependence of plants and animals is the basis for the branch of science called ecology. By learning about cells, the most basic units of life, we can begin to understand larger biological systems as a whole.

GLOSSARY

alveolus A microscopic air sac in the lungs that is lined with epithelial cells. The plural of alveolus is alveoli.

amino acid Any one of many acids that occur naturally in living things and that include some which form proteins.

autotrophic Needing only carbon dioxide or carbonates as a source of carbon and a simple inorganic nitrogen compound for metabolic synthesis.

cell The smallest unit of living matter that can exist by itself.

cell wall A rigid wall outside the cell membrane of plant cells. Composed mostly of cellulose, it provides support and protection.

cellular respiration The process by which organisms use oxygen to break down food molecules to get chemical energy for cell functions.

chloroplast A plastid that contains the pigment chlorophyll; it provides the site of photosynthesis.

chromoplast A plastid that contains carotenoid pigments.

cytoplasm A jellylike material that fills all the spaces in a cell between the plasma membrane and the nucleus.

cytoskeleton A meshlike network in the cytoplasm that provides internal support for the cells, anchors internal cell structures, and functions in cell movement and division.

deoxyribonucleic acid A substance that carries genetic information in the cells of plants and animals. Generally known by its abbreviation, DNA.

endoplasmic reticulum Long, stringy structures in eukaryotic cells where some proteins and lipids are synthesized and detoxification happens.

epithelial tissue Tissue that covers a free surface or lines a tube or cavity of an animal body and serves especially to enclose and protect the other parts of the body, to produce secretions and excretions, and to function in assimilation.

eukaryotic Having a distinct nucleus and intracellular membranes. All protists, fungi, plants, and animals are eukaryotic.

Golgi complex An organelle that handles protein processing and transport.

hemoglobin The part of blood that contains iron, carries oxygen through the body, and gives blood its red color

lysosome An organelle full of enzymes that enables a cell to break down certain molecules for recycling and disposal.

mitochondrion An organelle that serves as the site for the reaction of oxygen and glucose to produce energy used for the cell. The plural of "mitochon-drion" is "mitochondria."

neuron A very long, thin, wirelike cell, along which nerve signals pass from one part of the body to another.

nucleolus A round body inside the nucleus, which produces RNA that is sent out of the nucleus to other parts of the cell. The plural of "nucleolus" is "nucleoli."

nucleus A part of a cell containing DNA and RNA and responsible for growth and reproduction. The plural of "nucleus" is "nuclei."

organelle A structure inside a cell's cytoplasm that carries out a particular function in the life of the cell.

organism An individual living thing.

phloem tissue Cells of the vascular system in plants that transport food from leaves to other areas of the plant.

photosynthesis A chemical reaction in which energy from sunlight is harnessed and used to convert carbon dioxide and water into organic compounds—namely sugar molecules—and oxygen.

plasma membrane A thin, semipermeable double layer of fatty molecules that surrounds every cell.

plastid A kind of organelle in the cytoplasm of a plant cell.

prokaryotic Possessing no distinct nucleus, such as bacteria and cyanobacteria.

protein Any of various naturally occurring extremely complex substances that consist of amino-acid residues joined by peptide bonds and include many essential biological compounds (as enzymes, hormones, or antibodies).

ribosome An organelle, usually found on the surface of the endoplasmic reticulum, that functions in the synthesis of proteins.

stimulus Something that causes something else to happen, develop, or become more active. The plural of stimulus is stimuli.

tissue A group of similar cells that work together to carry out a specific function.

transpiration The process in which water passes through a plant.

vacuole A large sac in the inside of plant cells that removes waste products and stores food.

xylem tissue Tissue in the vascular system of plants that moves water and dissolved nutrients from the roots to the leaves.

FOR MORE INFORMATION

The American Society for Cell Biology
8120 Woodmont Avenue, Suite 750
Bethesda, MD 20814
(301) 347-9300
Website: http://www.ascb.org
The ASCB's mission statement affirms that it is "an inclu-
sive, international community of biologists studying
the cell, the fundamental unit of life." The group
includes more than 9,000 scientists, in more than
sixty-five countries. It offers career development,
awards prizes, and publishes several journals.

American Society for Microbiology
1752 N Street NW
Washington, DC 20036
(202) 737-3600
Website: http:///www.asm.org
First founded in 1899, the American Society for
Microbiology can lay claim to being the oldest
and largest single life science membership
organization in the world. Members must be interested in microbiology and have at least a
bachelor's degree in microbiology or a related
field. Despite the group's name, its membership
is not limited to Americans or those living in the
United States.

American Society of Plant Biologists
15501 Monona Drive
Rockville, MD 20855
(301) 251-0560

Website: http://my.aspb.org

This professional organization for plant scientists publishes two journals, organizes conferences, and presents several different awards. Its members include scientists specializing in fields such as cellular and molecular biology, genetics, development, evolution, physiology, and biochemistry.

The Botanical Society of America
4475 Castleman Avenue
St. Louis, MO 63110
(314) 577-9566
Website: http://botany.org

Formed in 1893, the Botanical Society of America seeks to promote botany, the study of plants, at all levels. Its membership consists of scientists, professors, teachers, students, and botanists, as well as non-professionals who happen to be interested in botany and plants.

The California Science Center
700 Exposition Park Drive
Los Angeles, CA 90037
(323) 724-3623
Website: http://www.californiasciencecenter.org

This Southern California museum aims to "to stimulate curiosity and inspire science learning in everyone by creating fun, memorable experiences." It has exhibits about a wide range of scientific topics. Its education arm is known as the Amgen Center for Science Learning.

Canadian Society for Molecular Biosciences
c/o Rofail Conference and Management Services (RCMS)
17 Dossetter Way
Ottawa, ON K1G 4S3
Canada
(613) 421-7229
Website: http://csmb-scbm.ca
This group was formed in 1957, with the goal of furthering
    the science of biochemistry. It presents awards,
    hosts conferences, publishes a journal, and holds
    annual meetings.

The Environmental Protection Agency
1200 Pennsylvania Avenue NW
Washington, DC 20460
(202) 272-0167
Website: http://www.epa.gov
This is the branch of the U.S. government that is in charge
    of enforcing environmental policy. As such, it is in
    charge of American government efforts to deal with
    the problem of global warming. The agency's infor-
    mative website has lots of facts about global warming,
    pollution, and associated topics.

Field Museum of Natural History
1400 S. Lake Shore Drive
Chicago, IL 60605
(312) 922-9410
Website: http://www.fieldmuseum.org
The Field Museum was an outgrowth of the World's
    Columbian Exposition, which was held in Chicago

in 1893. Today, it is both a museum and a research institution. The museum has vast collections and is a great place to learn about the variety of life on Earth.

The International Academy of Cytology
Office of the Secretary-Treasurer
Fernando Schmitt, MD, PhD, FIAC
P.O. Box 1347
79013 Freiburg i.Br.
Germany
+49 761 292 3801
Website: http://www.cytology-iac.org
This international organization of cytopathologists, cytotechnologists, and other professionals in the field of clinical cytology was formed in 1957. The group presents several awards for excellence in the field each year, including the International Cytotechnologist of the Year Award and the Maurice Goldblatt Cytology Award.

The Ontario Science Centre
770 Don Mills Road
Toronto, ON M3C 1T3
Canada
(416) 696-1000
Website: https://www.ontariosciencecentre.ca
This science museum's innovative interactive approach has made it a hit with the public since it opened in 1969. It has dozens of programs for students that tie

in with Ontario's science and technology curriculum. It even hosts sleepovers and birthday parties!

The Smithsonian Science Education Center
901 D Street SW, Suite 704B
Washington, DC 20024
(202) 633-2972
Website: http://www.ssec.si.edu
This organization was jointly established by the Smithsonian Institution and the National Academies. Its mission is to improve the teaching and learning of science around the world, and particularly in the United States. It was formerly known as the National Science Resource Center.

WEBSITES

Because of the changing nature of Internet links, Rosen Publishing has developed an online list of websites related to the subject of this book. This site is updated regularly. Please use this link to access this list:

http://www.rosenlinks.com/BGCB/Plant

FOR FURTHER READING

Calhoun, Yael. *Plant and Animal Science Fair Projects* (Biology Science Projects Using the Scientific Method). Berkeley Heights, NJ: Enslow Publishers, 2010.

Dowdy, Penny. *Plant Cells* (Let's Relate to Genetics). New York, NY: Crabtree Publishing, 2009.

Green, Jen. *Inside Animals* (Invisible Worlds). Tarrytown, NY: Benchmark Books, 2010.

Hopkins, William G. *Photosynthesis and Respiration* (The Green World). New York, NY: Chelsea House Publishers, 2006.

Johnson, Lori. *Cell Function and Specialization* (Sci-Hi: Life Science). Mankato, MN: Heinemann-Raintree, 2009.

Katz, Nevin. *Dr. Birdley Teaches Science: Introducing Cells.* Nashville, TN: Incentive Publications, 2007.

Latham, Donna. *Cells, Tissues, and Organs* (Sci-Hi: Life Science). Mankato, MN: Heinemann-Raintree, 2009.

Latham, Donna. *Respiration and Photosynthesis* (Sci-Hi: Life Science). Mankato, MN: Heinemann-Raintree, 2009.

Lee, Kimberly Fekany. *Cell Scientists: Discovering How Cells Work* (Science Readers: Life Science). Huntington Beach, CA: Teacher Created Materials, 2008.

Macceca, Michael L. *The World of Plants* (Science Readers: Life Science). Huntington Beach, CA: Teacher Created Materials, 2008.

Meredith, Susan. *Cells* (Let's Explore Science). Vero Beach, FL: Rourke Educational Media, 2009.

Marsh, Carol. *Christina Examines Plant Cells and Animal Cells* (Science Alliance). Peachtree City, GA: Gallopade International, 2008.

Newman, Michael E. *Cells and Human Health* (Cells: The Building Blocks of Life). New York, NY: Chelsea House Publishers, 2012.

Silverstein, Alvin, Virginia Silverstein, and Laura Silverstein Nunn. *Cells* (Science Concepts Second). Minneapolis, MN: Twenty-First Century Books, 2009.

Somervill, Barbara A. *Animal Cells and Life Processes* (Investigating Cells). Mankato, MN: Heinemann-Raintree, 2010.

Somervill, Barbara A. *Plant Cells and Life Processes* (Investigating Cells). Mankato, MN: Heinemann-Raintree, 2010.

Stimola, Aubrey. *Cell Biology* (Science Made Simple). New York, NY: Rosen Central, 2011.

Takemura, Masaharu, Sakura, and Becom Co. Ltd. *The Manga Guide to Molecular Biology.* San Francisco, CA: No Starch Press, 2009.

INDEX